LEADER'S GUIDE

God's Girl

DISCOVERING ME • KNOWING GOD • MAKING FRIENDS

Beth Hey

Copyright 2021 by Beth Hey
Triumph Literary Communications, LLC

Published by Comet Tale Books—an imprint of Electric Moon Publishing, LLC

©2021 *God's Girl: Discovering Me, Knowing God, Making Friends* / Beth Hey

Paperback ISBN: 978-1-955707-02-2
E-book ISBN: 978-1-955707-03-9

Electric Moon Publishing, LLC
P.O. Box 466
Stromsburg, NE 68666
info@emoonpublishing.com

All rights reserved. No part of this publication may be reproduced, distributed, or transmitted in any form or by any means, including photocopying, recording, or other electronic or mechanical methods, without the prior written permission of the publisher, except in the case of brief quotations embodied in critical reviews and certain other noncommercial uses permitted by copyright law. For permission requests, write to the publisher.

The opinions and quotations of the author are not necessarily that of the publisher or its affiliates/contractors/printers. Author retains all intellectual property rights. Contact author for questions or disputes.

Scripture quotations marked (NIV) are taken from the *Holy Bible, New International Version*®, NIV®. Copyright © 1973, 1978, 1984, 2011 by Biblica, Inc.™ Used by permission of Zondervan. All rights reserved worldwide. www.zondervan.com The "NIV" and "New International Version" are trademarks registered in the United States Patent and Trademark Office by Biblica, Inc.™

Scripture quotations are taken from the Holy Bible, New Living Translation, copyright © 1996, 2004, 2007 by Tyndale House Foundation. Used by permission of Tyndale House Publishers, Inc., Carol Stream, IL 60188. All rights reserved.

Cover created by Jennifer Stewart @Hello Joy! Co. Find her designs at *hellojoyco.com*.

Cover and Interior Design by Lyn Rayn / Electric Moon Publishing Creative Services

Printed in the United States of America

www.emoonpublishing.com

Thank you for leading your girl, or group of girls, through *God's Girl*!

I'm passionate about seeing women live out of their authentic self and become all they're created to be; it's the journey I've been on and continue to pursue today. I believe there's no better time to start the conversation and establish these pivotal concepts than in the middle school years! Since you've chosen to lead this Bible study, I'm confident you share a similar desire and vision:

To come alongside the next generation as they learn to exercise their faith and make their way in this challenging world of ours.

I pray that each topic will be a catalyst for self-discovery, discussion, and growth. *Look in the Mirror* quizzes and interactive questions create space for honest conversation and transparency. Chapters are designed to be completed in 30 to 40 minutes, depending on discussion length. Please use this leader's guide as it best suits your needs when preparing and as a reference when discussing the chapters with your girl or group of girls.

Let's get started!

Contents

Unpacking the Chapter Sections 7
Suggestions For Groups 11
The First Meeting—Introducing *God's Girl* 13

Chapter Overviews + Suggested Questions &
Discussion for Facilitation

Me

Week 1: Me? My Own Best Friend? 17
Week 2: Your Internal Chat 23
Week 3: Girl Power! 29

God

Week 4: God—My Heavenly Father? 37
Week 5: The Real Me 43
Week 6: Growing in God 49

Friends

Week 7: Faithful Friends 57
Week 8: Conquering Conflict 63
Week 9: Forgiveness—Path to Peace 69

Wrap It Up

Unpacking the Chapter Sections

When studying each chapter, it works well to read the sections aloud. Reading aloud keeps everyone focused and together, which can be done in a variety of ways. You can ask for volunteers, with each girl reading her section when it's her turn. Another option is to assign sections or paragraphs to different girls, or simply go around the circle.

Week 1
AS AN EXAMPLE
(Page numbers refer to pages in *God's Girl* Bible study.)

- *Opening Story* (p. 13)
    - For short stories, ask for a volunteer to read them aloud.
    - For longer stories (pp. 49–50), involve several volunteers—one for the first paragraph and readers for each of the six families described.
    - After each story, you might ask, *Can you relate to this story? Why or why not?*

- *What About You?* (p. 14)
    - The quiz should be completed individually.
    - Afterward, invite feedback.

- If your girl is willing to share, go through each question and find out how she answered. For groups, ask several girls to share a key insight they received.
- Finally, have someone read the concluding thoughts related to the quiz.

- *Digging Deeper* (pp. 14–15)
  - It's helpful to do this exercise together by reading the text and questions aloud and giving your girl(s) time to write a response.
  - Ask your girl(s) to share what she wrote and why.

- *Heart-to-Heart* (pp. 15–16)
  - Recommendation: Do this exercise together.
  - Ask one or two girls to read aloud.
  - Invite your girl(s) to ask questions or make comments while doing the exercise.

- *Scriptures* (p. 16)
  - Have your girl(s) look up the scripture with a phone or in a Bible. Read it aloud while your girl(s) fills in the blanks.
  - When complete, have someone reread the scripture aloud.

- *Look in the Mirror* (pp. 17–18)
  - The quiz should be completed individually.
  - First, explain how to take the quiz and how to score.
  - Give your girl(s) time to answer and tally it up.
  - As time permits, ask your girl(s) to share any insight she received.
  - Carefully gauge the level of transparency and trust. Share and talk about the scores accordingly.

- *Prayers* (pp. 18–19)
  - Ask for a volunteer to read the prayer.
  - Allow several minutes for each girl to write a personal prayer that she won't be asked to share.

- *Walk It Out* (pp. 20–21)
  - Read aloud each activity. Tell your girl(s) that this is an invitation to practice what has been learned.
  - Have your girl(s) share which specific one she will choose to focus on during the week.
  - The following week, begin the class by asking your girl(s) to share what she did. Sharing her experience each week will encourage accountability.

- *Wrap It Up* (pp. 115–116)
  - Picture this last section in the book as your girl's spiritual suitcase! Each week, she'll be adding a truth or discovery about herself that she wants to take along on her spiritual journey.
  - This space will help solidify what she has learned.
  - At the close of each weekly session, challenge your girl(s) to write down a significant truth or take-away that she wants to remember. She'll add it to the appropriate section: *Me, God,* or *Friends*.
  - As a guide, she can use two lines each week, which will help her be concise.

Suggestions for Group Study

- Decide when to divide your girls into smaller groups:
  - The size of your small group might vary depending on how comfortable the girls are with each other and how willing they are to share.
  - **Recommendation:** If you have six or seven girls, stay in one group. If you have more, divide them into groups based on the number of available leaders.
- Pass out materials: *God's Girl* study books, pens, and New Living Translation Bibles (for those who won't be using their smartphone to look up verses).
- Have each girl write her first and last name on the inside front cover.
- Let the girls know this Bible study is theirs to keep.
- Talk about the need for confidentiality so that everyone feels comfortable sharing.
- As the leader, decide how you want to manage their books during the study:
  - **Option 1:** Collect the books at the end of every session.
  Pro: Guarantees your girls will have their own books to write in each session.
  Con: You'll need to pass out a copy of the *Walk It Out* section (found at the end of every chapter), so each girl can do the activities at home during the upcoming week.

- **Option 2:** Girls take their book home and bring it back each week.
  Pro: No need to pass out a copy of the *Walk It Out* section each week.
  Con: If someone fails to bring her book, she won't be able to fill out the chapter during group time.
- **Option 3:** Give each girl a choice to take her book home or leave it with you.
  Pro: Some girls may want to spend more time with the topic during the week.
  Con: You'll need to pass out a copy of the *Walk It Out* section to the girls who don't take their book home. For those who take their book home, they'll need to remember to bring it back.

Note:
From this point forward, and for simplicity, I'll refer to one girl or a group of girls as "your girl."

The First Meeting—
Introducing God's Girl

Getting Started:
- Let your girl know how excited you are to start this study with her! She'll be digging into scripture, taking self-discovery quizzes, and choosing activities. They will help reveal what she thinks and how she feels about herself, how she relates to others, and ways to know God better. As a bonus, Week One, Four, and Nine include coloring pages.
- Tell your girl this is her personal study book, so she can answer honestly and have fun!
- For a group study, ask each girl to introduce herself and share a one-sentence, fun fact about herself. (As the leader, you set the tone of the study; share first and create an atmosphere of fun and authenticity!)

Have your girl turn to the *Contents* page:
- This study is divided into three sections: *Me, God, Friends.*
- Read through all the chapter titles to let her know what topics will be covered.

Have your girl turn to the *Forward* on page 9:
- Read the *Forward* aloud or ask for a volunteer.
- Emphasize the importance of attending weekly if possible.
- Remind her that by simply showing up, God will bless her through the study.
- Challenge your girl to share openly and honestly. Reinforce that you'll respect her comfort level.
- If this is a group study, remind your girls that they can encourage and strengthen each other in their walk with God by being transparent. Your girls will also discover they're not alone in their struggles.

Have your girl turn to the *Introduction* and *You're Invited* on page 11:
- Read both sections aloud or ask for volunteers.
- If this is a group setting, go around the circle having the girls read aloud *Who? What? Where?* etc., or alternate reading aloud if this is a one-on-one study.

Let her know that:
- There will be scriptures to look up and fill-in-the-blanks using the New Living Translation Bible.
- Remind her that all answers are personal and don't have to be shared unless she chooses to do so during discussion time.
- Every chapter ends with *Walk It Out* suggestions that offer activity choices for the week ahead. The goal is to experience and practice the truths that she's studied and discussed.

WEEK

— 1 —

OVERVIEW

Me? My Own Best Friend?

This week your girl will be unpacking how to love herself. While that might sound self-centered or particularly inward-focused, she'll find that it's actually scriptural! To authentically love others, your girl must be able to see herself from God's perspective first. The grace and dignity she learns to give herself can then be extended to others. By leaning into her own value and worth, she can move forward and become all God has created her to be.

In Mark 12:28–31, Jesus commands that we love our neighbor as ourselves. A seemingly simple command is attached to a very complex issue. Jesus implies that how we love ourselves is the model for how He wants us to love our neighbor. Buzzwords like self-esteem and self-love can have negative connotations. The idea of nurturing our hearts is sometimes viewed as either unnecessary or self-centered, but scripture teaches that nurturing and valuing ourselves is important.

Culture pushes against this idea of properly loving ourselves. In our social media–saturated world, the focus often lies on outer appearance and performance. But God has a very different assessment! He assigns value and worth based on who we *are*—rather than what we do or what we look like. Sure, it's important to be the best version of ourselves, but that's not what gives us worth from God's perspective.

What does it look like to be our own best friend? From the middle school years into our 20s, 30s, and beyond? Authentic love starts with putting aside our inner critic and learning to walk in grace, which we'll talk about in-depth next week. Grace, patience, and acceptance ought to be part of our renewed thinking. We can live knowing that our heavenly father is pleased with us. Wherever we find ourselves on this journey, as we grow in befriending and loving ourselves, it speaks volumes to those we influence!

While answering the *Look in the Mirror* quiz, your girl may realize that she's much harder on herself than she is on others. And if she didn't know it already, your girl might also discover that she's not alone in her struggles. The *Walk It Out* activity is designed to help your girl consistently speak truth to herself throughout the coming week—she is beloved, accepted, and valued. Remind her to deposit the *real* truth of who she is into her life every day. It's a battle not easily won but well worth the effort!

Week 1
SUGGESTED QUESTIONS & DISCUSSION FOR FACILITATION

Icebreaker: If you could create a new ice cream flavor, what would it be?

Leader Prays to Open

Opening Story (p. 13): Who would like to read the story aloud?

What About You? (p. 14): If you have a best friend, what is she like?

Digging Deeper (pp. 14–15): Why would God want us to first love ourselves?

Heart-to-Heart (pp. 15–16): Psalm 139 will be referred to in several chapters. You might want to take turns reading aloud Psalm 139 before your girl fills in the scripture on page 16. The message of this Psalm is important to this study because it describes how well God knows us and the great value He places on each person.

FOR FURTHER DISCUSSION

- ♥ What does Psalm 139 say to you?
- ♥ God values you. How does that make you feel? Is it easy or hard to believe?

Look in the Mirror (pp. 17–18):
- Are you surprised by your score? (Remind your girl that everyone finds it challenging to love and accept themselves, at least in some area!)
- What's your greatest struggle in accepting yourself?

FOR FURTHER DISCUSSION

- ♥ Is it hard to think of being a friend to yourself? Why?
- ♥ How can you be a better friend to yourself?

Prayer (pp. 18–19): Give your girl time to read the prayer and then to write her own prayer.

Walk It Out (pp. 20–21): Discuss the heart activity for this week. If time allows, have your girl start writing a character trait on each heart. Help her brainstorm if she needs some ideas.

Wrap It Up (p. 115): Turn to page 115 and introduce this section. Tell your girl it's like packing her suitcase for her spiritual journey. Each week before you close, she'll be invited to write one or two sentences in the corresponding sections—*Me, God,* and *Friends.* Hopefully, there will be a key truth from each week that she'll want to remember going forward.

- Point out the *Me* section, and invite her to write down one or two sentences about the most important truth she learned this week.

Notes

Notes

WEEK 2 OVERVIEW

Your Internal Chat

So how does your girl *Live Loved* as the coloring page suggests on page 23? This week, she'll dive into her thought life: how it affects her view of herself and her relationship with God. Putting aside that inner critic is a lifelong journey! And admittedly, that goal is more challenging for some personalities than for others. Your girl might not realize that loving herself starts with paying attention to her self-talk. What she says to herself can be quite revealing.

As your girl answers the *Look in the Mirror* section on page 27, is she aware of her internal dialogue and how it affects her? If she's open to discussing her self-talk, you might gently point out its influence. Maybe her self-talk is shaming or comparing: *I can't believe I did that!* or *Why can't I be like her?* Maybe she calls herself names: *I'm such an idiot!* or *I'm so stupid!* Maybe she's self-defeating: *I'll never be good enough.* Your girl might confess that she's kinder to a friend than she is to herself.

This chapter highlights verses that declare God's love for us. It's easy to gloss over often-quoted scriptures about God's deep and never-ending love. But God wants us to take them to heart—to meditate, or chew on, those scriptures and learn to receive His love. The value He places on us isn't tied to either our performance or our mistakes. Often, what we believe intellectually needs to become more deeply rooted at the heart level so that we actually live loved.

Believing what God says is a daily choice. Remind your girl to start paying attention to her self-talk. Challenge her to believe the truth about herself when her self-talk doesn't line up with God's opinion of her.

Week 2
SUGGESTED QUESTIONS & DISCUSSION FOR FACILITATION

Icebreaker: What is something you've made that you enjoyed creating? (artwork, a favorite meal, DIY, etc.)

Leader Prays to Open

Check In: What did you learn about yourself from last week's *Walk It Out* heart activity?

Opening Story (pp. 25–26): Who would like to read the story aloud?

What About You? (p. 26):
- Is self-talk something you've thought about before?
- Do you feel your self-talk is more positive or more negative?

Look in the Mirror (p. 27):
- Is self-talk something you do often?
- Do you accept yourself for who you are? Is that question easy or hard to answer?

FOR FURTHER DISCUSSION

♥ Why do we sometimes say things to ourselves that we would never say to a friend?

_____

Digging Deeper (pp. 28–30):
- How do you compare the way you love yourself with the love described in Ephesians 4:2?
- Would you be willing to share where you struggle with self-acceptance?

Heart-to-Heart (pp. 30–31):
- How do you feel when you've made something you're proud of and then someone criticizes it? (That gives us a small taste of what God probably feels when we criticize ourselves. When we beat ourselves up, we're complaining about what God created.)

Transform: Refer to the box at the bottom of page 30. How might your self-talk change when you see yourself as God sees you?

FOR FURTHER DISCUSSION

♥ In what practical ways can you love yourself? See what your girl answers and add to her list. Discuss . . .

- Giving ourselves grace.
- How expectations from ourselves and others play into being self-critical.
- Ditching comparison—discuss how pride or shame is often the result of comparison.
- Setting a "high bar" that's difficult to achieve.
- Talk about God's value system; our value and worth are not based on what we do or achieve.

———————

Prayer (p. 32): Give your girl time to read the prayer and then to write her own prayer.

Walk It Out (p. 33): Discuss the activities and ask your girl to pick one she would like to do this week.

Wrap It Up (p. 115): Turn to page 115. Under the *Me* section, invite her to write one or two sentences about the most important truth she learned this week.

Notes

WEEK 3 OVERVIEW

Girl Power!

This week, your girl will gain a better understanding of who she is as a female created in God's image. Genesis 2:21-23 says that God took Eve out of Adam's side. In other words, up to that moment, Adam contained all humankind—both male and female. But God decided to show different aspects of Himself through Adam *and* Eve. The first man and woman had many characteristics that were the same, but their roles weren't necessarily the same. Together, Adam and Eve reflected the complete picture of God.

In the original language of Genesis 2:18, Eve was created to be an *ezer* to Adam. In the Bible, that word is translated as *helper*, which connotes weakness. But the Hebrew word *ezer*, in the language of the Old Testament, is primarily used to describe God's relationship to humankind as our helper or lifesaver. An *ezer* describes someone of strength—who rescues, who protects, and sustains another.

God used a description for women that He used for Himself! That's who God destined Eve to be—brave and resilient to serve alongside man as his equal. For instance, in Deuteronomy 33:29 (NIV), "Blessed are you, O Israel! Who is like you, a people saved by the LORD? He is your shield and *helper* and your glorious sword." And in Psalm 33:20 (NIV), "We wait in hope for the LORD; he is our *help* and our shield." Clearly, the word translated *helper* in the Bible should not be misinterpreted for weakness!

Today, gender is increasingly precarious to discuss. Your girl's gender—her femaleness—is significant to her true self. Now, more than ever, it's essential to reinforce the blueprint set forth in the book of Genesis. For the majority of girls, who aren't wrestling with serious gender questions, explore what it means to be uniquely female while acknowledging the vast differences in personality, preferences, and desires. Your girl is looking for affirmation in her identity, part of which includes her feminine heart.

Note:
If your girl is struggling with gender identity, it's important to truly listen. Dialogue with her. Thank her for being willing to share the struggle she is facing. Ask about the adults in her life: Are they aware? Does she have a pastor or another trusted resource that she can talk to?

Week 3
SUGGESTED QUESTIONS & DISCUSSION FOR FACILITATION

Icebreaker: What quality or trait do you like most about yourself? Why?

Leader Prays to Open

Check In: Which activity did you pick from last week's *Walk It Out* section? How did it go?

Opening Story (p. 35): Who would like to read the story aloud?

What About You? (pp. 36–37): Talk about each question and find out where your girl is coming from.

Digging Deeper (pp. 37–38): Do you agree that, according to the Bible, men and women together reflect the whole image of God? Why or why not?

FOR FURTHER DISCUSSION

♥ Share the Hebrew word for *helper*, found in Genesis 2:18, which is *ezer*. This word refers to someone who is strong, rescues, protects, and helps. It describes fierceness and goes way beyond our contemporary connotation of simply helping someone.

Heart-to-Heart (pp. 39–44):
You're a Relationship Builder (pp. 39–40)
- What did you check on page 40? How do you like to spend time with your friends?

FOR FURTHER DISCUSSION

♥ How important are your friends and relationships? What makes them so important to you?

_____

You're a Beauty Bringer (pp. 40–43)
- Let's talk about beauty. What makes someone beautiful?

FOR FURTHER DISCUSSION

♥ Talk about what makes someone beautiful—their inner qualities and not necessarily their outward appearance. Have your girl share her experiences. Has she known someone who might be beautiful on the outside but not on the inside?

_____

You're a Life Giver (pp. 43–44)
- Who is an example of a good leader in your life?
- Is there someone you know who has been a life giver in other ways? What did they do?

FOR FURTHER DISCUSSION

♥ How is being brave life giving?

♥ How is courage part of being a good leader? Talk about resisting peer pressure, including someone outside of her social circle or standing up for someone being bullied.

Look in the Mirror (pp. 44–45):
- From these questions, describe how you're a life giver to others?
- What areas of serving do you need to grow in?

Prayer (p. 46): Give your girl time to read the prayer and then to write her own prayer.

Walk It Out (p. 47): Which of the three—relationship builder, beauty bringer, or life giver—would you like to focus on this week?

Wrap It Up (p. 115): Turn to page 115. Under the *Me* section, invite her to write one or two sentences about the most important truth she learned this week.

WEEK 4 OVERVIEW

God . . . My Heavenly Father?

This week, your girl will be exploring her experience with her earthly dad and her heavenly father. The *Look in the Mirror* quizzes will help your girl think about both relationships. Evaluating these two relationships might be familiar territory, or this topic might bring up new thoughts and feelings.

Wherever it lands on the spectrum, the relationship and experience with our earthly dad have deeply influenced us. Our perception of God as a trustworthy, good, and loving father has been influenced by our earthly relationships! The connection might be obvious between the emotions and thoughts surrounding our earthly dad and our heavenly father, or it might be more subtle.

How we interpret our reality holds weight! Sometimes, the stories we tell ourselves about God are accurate and other times not so much. We all have incorrect perceptions about God and, therefore, struggle to trust Him fully. Only the Holy Spirit can change those false images that have been planted and rooted in our heart and mind. Thankfully, our heavenly father is more than patient to show Himself to us.

This chapter ends with an invitation for your girl to accept Christ. Let her know that this invitation is always extended and involves individual choice! It's important not to assume that your girl, particularly if she's in a group, has a correct understanding of salvation and is saved. Don't skip over this section. Hopefully, the highlighted scriptures and questions will open the door to honest dialogue about your girl's spiritual journey.

Week 4
SUGGESTED QUESTIONS & DISCUSSION FOR FACILITATION

Icebreaker: Describe your favorite vacation or place you've visited.

Leader Prays to Open

Check In: Which area did you focus on in last week's *Walk It Out* section—relationship builder, beauty bringer, or life giver? What did you learn about yourself?

Opening Story (pp. 49–50): Who would like to read the story aloud?

What About You? (pp. 50–51):
- Was there a dad or family situation that you related to? Which one?
- What about that situation is similar to your own life?

Look in the Mirror (pp. 51–52):
- What did you score on the earthly dad quiz?
- What did you score on the heavenly father quiz?
- How do your two scores compare?

FOR FURTHER DISCUSSION

♥ Is this a new idea . . . the way you relate to or view God, as your heavenly father, is often the way you have related to your earthly dad?

———————

Digging Deeper (pp. 52–55):
- What did you circle in Exodus 34:5–7?
- What do these verses in Psalms and Exodus say about God as our heavenly father?

FOR FURTHER DISCUSSION

♥ Have you had words of encouragement and affirmation spoken to you by your parents, teacher, or another adult whose opinion you respect?

♥ What does it mean to have God's blessing?

♥ In Romans 8:15–16, what does being called God's daughter mean to you?

♥ Ephesians 2:8–9 talks about God's grace. What is grace?
- Something we don't earn, not based on performance
- Freely given by God
- "Grace is God acting in our life to do what we cannot do on our own." —Dallas Willard

———————

Heart-to-Heart (pp. 55–56): Revelation 3:20 tells your girl that she can choose to have a relationship with Jesus. Discuss the fact that the doorknob is on the inside of her heart. And, as a Christian, she still has the choice to invite Him into her life every day and ask Him to be involved in everything she does.

- Where are you in your spiritual journey? (Depending on your girl's comfort level to share, ask her where she is in her decision to follow Christ—see top of page 56.)
- Discuss being real before God because He knows our hearts already. She might want to rededicate her life to God if she accepted Him at a young age.

Prayer (p. 56): If your girl wants to accept Christ into her heart, ask if she would like to pray each sentence after you so that she can think about the words. Or she can pray on her own.

Walk It Out (p. 57): Refer to Psalm 139. Ask your girl which activity she wants to do this week.

Wrap It Up (p. 115): Turn to page 115. Under the *God* section, invite her to write one or two sentences about the most important truth she learned this week.

Notes

Notes

WEEK 5 OVERVIEW

The Real Me

This week, your girl is going to take a closer look at her identity. Identity answers the questions *Who am I?* and *Whose am I?* Many things can shape identity, and she'll take time to evaluate those good and not-so-good influences.

She'll also look at identity from God's viewpoint and be challenged where her thinking doesn't line up with who God says she is. Sometimes, lies and false ideas keep her from accepting herself and from viewing herself rightly. She can break their power by renouncing the lies and beginning to replace them with God's truth (see the prayer on page 66).

As followers of Christ, God desires that our identity be rooted in Him. We are God's masterpiece, adopted into His family, without condemnation, and righteous because of Christ's payment for our sins. That's a lot to take in! But understanding all that has been done for us is critical to seeing ourselves as God sees us.

In the messiness of life and relationships, shame and condemnation get in the way of right believing. Our reality isn't dependent on external things, accomplishments, successes or failures, how others perceive us, or what we think about ourselves. We cannot do more to gain God's approval and love! It's a conscious decision to believe that we are "holy and dearly loved," as Paul states in Colossians 3:12.

Whether the concepts in this chapter are new or truths that your girl already might know, your girl needs to own them for herself at a heart level. As these truths become planted in her heart, it will go far in helping her withstand the pressures that she continually faces.

How does your girl accept her God-given identity? Jesus listened to the voice of His father, who spoke affirmation and blessing over Him. She, too, must focus on the influences that speak truth into her life. With the help of the Holy Spirit, she can battle the lies that she believes. She can acknowledge that righteousness and God's love can't be earned, only received. Your girl can accept the invitation to believe who God says she is in Christ.

Week 5
SUGGESTED QUESTIONS & DISCUSSION FOR FACILITATION

Icebreaker: If you could be any animal in the world, which one would you choose and why?

Leader Prays to Open

Check In: How did your *Walk It Out* activity go this past week? What did you learn about yourself?

Opening Story (p. 61): Who would like to read the story aloud?

What About You? (pp. 62–63):
- What are your top three good influences?
- What are your top three not-so-good influences?
- Do you have other good and not-so-good influences?

Digging Deeper (p. 63):
- What does identity mean to you?
- How does your identity affect and influence your life?

Look in the Mirror (pp. 64–65): From the quiz, what has defined you the most?

Heart-to-Heart (pp. 65–68):
- Is there a lie, like Emily's or something completely different, that you've believed about yourself or about God? Can you name that lie or lies?

If there's a lie your girl wants to deal with, you can offer ministry either in the group or individually. If your girl is willing, she can use the prayer on page 66, name the lie, and break its authority over her. There's something powerful about verbally breaking the lie aloud and having someone else witness it. But, if she prefers to pray on her own, that's fine too. Let her know that this prayer is one she can pray every time the lie comes up, especially if it's lodged deep within her. Remind your girl that victory will come!

FOR FURTHER DISCUSSION

- ♥ What is faith? Can you describe it in your own words?
- ♥ Do you agree or disagree that you can do things to grow your faith? (If she says *yes*, ask her how she would like to exercise her faith—see suggestions on page 68.)

Prayer (pp. 68–69): Give your girl time to read the prayer and then to write her own prayer.

Walk It Out (p. 70): Discuss the activities and ask your girl which one she wants to focus on this week.

Wrap It Up (p. 115): Turn to page 115. Under the *God* section, invite her to write one or two sentences about the most important truth she learned this week.

Notes

Notes

WEEK 6 OVERVIEW

Growing in God

This week, your girl will look at ways that she can develop a deeper relationship with God. What does it mean to be a disciple of Christ? The term *disciple* may seem old-fashioned, but it simply means to be an active follower and learner of Christ.

There's a continual battle for our heart! Some of that battle is within our own flesh. But we also have a real adversary in Satan. In John 8:44, Jesus calls him the "father of lies." It's important to recognize that there is opposition when we say "yes" to God. Satan doesn't want us to become all God has envisioned for us from our beginning, and Satan will try to stop our growth. We can also stunt our spiritual maturity by not making the effort to pursue God. As we exercise our will and choose to follow God and spend time with Him, we open ourselves to the Holy Spirit who can transform our life.

This chapter will probably challenge your girl, but the seeds planted here will bring future growth. Worship, reading the Bible, and prayer will help her connect with God. In addition, you can stimulate that growth by asking God to help your girl become more aware of His presence in everyday circumstances.

Week 6
SUGGESTED QUESTIONS & DISCUSSION FOR FACILITATION

Icebreaker: What's your favorite hobby or go-to activity in your spare time?

Leader Prays to Open

Check In: Which activity did you do in the *Walk It Out* section? What did you learn about your identity and the influences in your life?

Opening Story (pp. 71–72): Who would like to read the story aloud?

What About You? (p. 72):
- Of all the ways you deal with being upset, stressed, or fearful, what's your most common response?
- What didn't you check and why?

Look in the Mirror (pp. 73–74):
- How do you deal with difficult situations? What did you check?

FOR FURTHER DISCUSSION

♥ *Disciple*: Refer to the box at the bottom of page 73. Talk about what it means to be a disciple. God has already done His part through Jesus' life, death, and resurrection. Now it's our turn to respond. A disciple isn't someone who just talks about Jesus but who obeys Him and walks it out. God invites us to become lifelong learners of Christ and to have both a relationship and friendship with Him. We, in turn, choose our response to His invitation.

♥ In Colossians 2:6-7, three actions in this verse build on each other . . .
- What happens first?
- After we accept Christ, what must we do next?
- Finally, what happens as we build our lives on Christ?

♥ For you personally, is this a new understanding of what it means to be a disciple?

♥ Based on what we've just talked about, are you a disciple of Jesus, or do you want to be?

Digging Deeper (pp. 74–75): Discuss growing stronger in God and developing "roots" in God. You might want to introduce Psalm 1 and Jeremiah 17:7-8 that use the example of a tree to picture a life rooted in God. Why would these verses use a tree as a metaphor for life in God?

Heart-to-Heart (pp. 75–77): This section describes ways to grow strong roots.
- Find out if any of these resonate with your girl . . .

    1. Sing Songs to God: How do you feel when you worship?
       Does worship refresh you and connect you more closely to God? Why or why not?
    2. Read the Bible: Why is it important to read the Bible?
       What make reading the Bible enjoyable for you? (Discuss the ideas presented in this study and any others you or your girl might suggest.)
    3. Spend a few minutes praying: What is prayer? (Refer to the definition of prayer in the box on p. 77)
       Have you ever asked God to talk to you? What happened?

FOR FURTHER DISCUSSION

♥ Which of these—worship, reading the Bible, or prayer—is the most challenging for you? Any thoughts as to why?

_____

Prayer (p. 78): Give your girl time to read the prayer and then to write her own prayer.

Walk It Out (p. 79): Read through the activities for worship, reading the Bible, and prayer. Ask your girl to pick one area for this week and why she is choosing that particular activity.

Wrap It Up (p. 115): Turn to page 115. Under the *God* section, invite her to write one or two sentences about the most important truth she learned this week.

Notes

WEEK
— 7 —
OVERVIEW

Faithful Friends

This week, your girl will dive into one of her favorite topics—friendships. Those all-important peer relationships at the center of her world, bringing a sense of belonging and laughter and fun into her life! However, they can also cause anxiety and unresolved conflict. First, we'll unpack what makes a good friendship before we focus on relational conflict and ways to navigate it in the next two chapters.

Most likely, your girl will have much to share about her best friend and why their friendship works! Hopefully, that conversation will be a springboard to discussing real-life situations that occur and how she can choose to react to them. In the *Heart-to-Heart* section, she'll look at some of the secrets to nurturing authentic friendships.

Choosing friends who encourage us, especially spiritually, is key to growing in God! As Proverbs 13:20 reminds us, our community of friends influences us in subtle and not-so-subtle ways. Talking about "red flags" in relationships will probably bring up some real-life scenarios that your girl has experienced. If the discussion warrants, Proverbs 16:28 and 17:9 also address conflict and gossip.

Just as important as cultivating her current friendships is your girl's ability to befriend others. She'll take a look at what it means to accept and value others and read what scripture says about being a good friend. Challenging her to serve—to step out and love unconditionally in practical ways—might go a bit beyond her comfort zone. With this in mind, the *Walk It Out* section offers hands-on ideas to serve in the week ahead.

Week 7
SUGGESTED QUESTIONS & DISCUSSION FOR FACILITATION

Icebreaker: If you could plan the perfect Friday night with your best friend, what would you do?

Leader Prays to Open

Check In: Which activity did your girl focus on last week—worship, reading the Bible, or prayer? How did it go?

Opening Story (pp. 81-82): Who would like to read the story aloud?

What About You? (pp. 82-83): What do you like most about your best friend?

Look in the Mirror (pp. 83-84): Based on how you answered the quiz, what kind of friend are you?

Digging Deeper (pp. 85–86):
- Have you seen situations where you (or someone else) became like the person or group that you (or they) hung out with?
- Have you experienced a "red flag" in a friendship?
- What was that "red flag?"
- Did you pay attention to it?
- What happened in that situation?

Heart-to-Heart (pp. 86–87):
- Do you have a friend like the one described in these verses?
- She may or may not have all of these qualities, but which ones does she have?
- Are you this kind of friend to someone else?

FOR FURTHER DISCUSSION

♥ What can you do to become a better friend?

♥ How will you pick your friends differently in the future based on what we've talked about this week?

Prayer (p. 87–88): Give your girl time to read the prayer and then to write her own prayer.

Walk It Out (p. 89): Read through the activities and have your girl pick one to do this week.

Wrap It Up (p. 116): Turn to page 116. Under the *Friends* section, invite her to write one or two sentences about the most important truth she learned this week.

Notes

Notes

WEEK 8 OVERVIEW

Conquering Conflict

This week, your girl will take a close look at the hot-button topic of conflict! Your girl will evaluate how she usually deals with it, compared to the three typical approaches described. She'll also gain some new ideas for handling conflict differently. The ability to deal with conflict in a healthy way is a skill that she'll use for the rest of her life, and it's one that is not easily mastered.

Conflict is messy! First, your girl will think about a current conflict in her own life—what is it and has she been able to resolve it? Then, she'll be invited to consider past scenarios that she experienced and how she approached those conflicts. The conversation might get somewhat animated or uncomfortable as she thinks about her unresolved conflicts. Remember that the goal is to give her ideas and tools to approach conflict differently, along with giving her much grace and time to mature. Dealing well with conflict remains a lifelong challenge.

Because we can't control another person's response, sometimes dealing well with conflict means setting healthy boundaries. This is a good time to discuss what boundaries are and positive ways to put them in place. Equally important is to discuss that our actions can also violate the boundaries of others and the need to respect those boundaries.

The key to conflict resolution is figuring out what drives the conflict. The root might be something obvious, or we might need to dig a bit deeper. Sometimes the solution will require us to take responsibility for our emotions and actions—which is often difficult! However, we aren't responsible for another person's actions, and even if we aren't in the wrong, we can still approach others in a respectful way that honors God.

Week 8
SUGGESTED QUESTIONS & DISCUSSION FOR FACILITATION

Icebreaker: If you had a superpower that allowed you to be amazing at one sport, what would it be and why?

Leader Prays to Open

Check In: Which activity did you focus on this past week? What did you learn about being a friend?

Opening Story (pp. 91-92): Who would like to read the story aloud?

What About You? (p. 92):
- Is the conflict you wrote down resolved?
- If so, are you happy with the outcome?

Digging Deeper (p. 93): Which of these three ways best describes how you handle conflict?

Look in the Mirror (pp. 94–97):
- Based on your real-life answers, how do you usually handle conflict?
- Why do you tend to handle conflict that way?

FOR FURTHER DISCUSSION

♥ Do you believe conflict starts in the heart? Why or why not?

_____

- p. 96-Possible Situations: Have your girl read each scenario aloud and discuss what emotion might be involved. (Hint: There's more than one answer in most situations.)

FOR FURTHER DISCUSSION

♥ Point out that anger is most often a secondary emotion—meaning there's usually another emotion that's driving the anger. For instance, a person who is afraid might get angry instead of acting fearful. Does your girl agree or disagree?

♥ Talk about the fact that no one can "make us mad." We choose to become angry. Does your girl agree or disagree with these statements?

––––––––––––––––

Heart-to-Heart (pp. 97–98):
- How does the picture of a fence help you to think about your boundaries and those of other people? (Refer to the definition of "Boundary" in the call-out box.)
- Do boundaries make sense to you? Why or why not?
- Have you crossed someone else's boundaries in the past? If so, what happened?
- Has someone crossed your boundaries? If so, what happened?
- What is an example of setting a healthy boundary in a friendship or relationship?

Prayer (p. 98–99): Give your girl time to read the prayer and then to write her own prayer.

Walk It Out (p. 100): Read through the activities and have your girl pick one to do this next week.

Wrap It Up (p. 116): Turn to page 116. Under the *Friends* section, invite her to write one or two sentences about the most important truth she learned this week.

WEEK 9 OVERVIEW

Forgiveness—Path to Peace

This week, your girl will continue looking at conflict and how to resolve it from a different perspective—that of forgiveness. Without forgiveness, it's often difficult or impossible to find a resolution! Many times, forgiveness is needed for a relationship to move forward. Forgiveness helps resolve the hurt that arises from the conflict, even if the conflict itself remains unresolved.

Like many of her peers, your girl might have misconceptions about forgiveness: How does it work? Why does it work? Who actually benefits? To begin, she'll take a *Look in the Mirror* quiz to pinpoint any misunderstandings.

Forgiveness starts the process of resolving our internal conflict, anger, or bitterness over a situation or relationship. Ultimately, forgiveness results in letting go and finding peace! It takes us out of the judgment seat. Sometimes, the forgiveness we need to extend is to ourselves. This is often the most difficult because we don't feel deserving, but Jesus' death on the cross covered every possibility and situation in life. In contrast, unforgiveness brings death to our souls. Peace is elusive because that situation replays over and over in our mind and heart.

However, just because forgiveness has taken place, reconciliation with the other person doesn't always happen—and sometimes shouldn't happen. Forgiveness can be the starting point to reconciling a relationship, but it doesn't guarantee reconciliation. In a relationship with numerous "red flags," caution is wise! In a damaging or abusive relationship, good boundaries are necessary. Trust may have been broken in a significant way. Each person must evaluate the particular relationship in question and seek wisdom about how to go forward.

Week 9
SUGGESTED QUESTIONS & DISCUSSION FOR FACILITATION

Icebreaker: What's the best gift that you have ever received?

Leader Prays to Open

Check In: During the week, did you talk to someone about a current conflict? If so, what happened? Or did you watch a movie and figure out the conflict? What did you learn?

Opening Story (pp. 101–102): Who would like to read the story aloud?

What About You? (pp. 102–103): What are the three ways to resolve conflict that we talked about last week?

Look in the Mirror (pp. 103–105): In the forgiveness quiz, are there any answers you disagree with? (It might be helpful to read each statement and discuss them one at a time.)

Heart-to-Heart (pp. 106–108): Praying to forgive someone is like putting our stake in the ground and saying, *I'm choosing to forgive.* Forgiveness is a process, and the prayer on page 106 can be a starting point. If your girl isn't willing to forgive yet, she can pray, *Lord, help me to want to forgive.* Equally powerful is forgiving ourselves and letting ourselves off the proverbial hook. See the prayer on page 107.

FOR FURTHER DISCUSSION

- ♥ Why is it sometimes hardest to forgive ourselves?
- ♥ When you've offended someone, do you agree or disagree that saying, *I'm sorry,* isn't as powerful as saying, *Will you forgive me?*
- ♥ What do you usually say?

Digging Deeper (pp. 109–110): Read the parable aloud and discuss the questions together.

FOR FURTHER DISCUSSION

- ♥ Was the king's punishment fair? Why or why not?
- ♥ What are some of the benefits of forgiveness?

- ♥ How would you describe forgiveness to someone else?
- ♥ Can you give an example of when you forgave someone?

Prayer (p. 111): Give your girl time to read the prayers.

Walk It Out (p. 112): Are you struggling to forgive someone, or are you struggling to forgive yourself? If either applies to you, then spend some time this week with one or both of these prayers.

Wrap It Up (p. 116): Turn to page 116. Under the *Friends* section, invite her to write one or two sentences about the most important truth she learned this week.

OVERVIEW

Wrap It Up

During the last session, ask your girl if she'd like to share any truths she wrote down during your time together. Wrap up by listening to her and discussing those significant truths she wants to apply on her journey going forward.

Notes

Notes

Notes

Thank you for choosing this study and for investing your time and energy in the next generation of God's girls!

Every blessing!

Beth

About Beth

Beth Hey has spent more than 20 years leading Bible studies and leading inner-healing ministries. She is passionate to see girls and women grow into their true identity in Christ and pursuing wholeness. During her writing career, her publishing credits have included Focus on the Family's *Clubhouse* and *Focus on Your Child-Tween* magazines. When not traveling, you can find Beth in her art studio dreaming up projects or getting dirt under her fingernails in her flower garden. She and her husband live in Kansas City and have three happily married children.

Follow Beth and her writing at bethheybooks.com.

Electric Moon Publishing, LLC is a custom, independent publisher who assists indie authors, ministries, businesses, and organizations with their book publishing needs. Services include writing, editing, design, layout, print, e-book, marketing, and distribution. For more information please use the contact form found on www.emoonpublishing.com.

www.ingramcontent.com/pod-product-compliance
Lightning Source LLC
Chambersburg PA
CBHW081311070526
44578CB00006B/842